Low Calorie C

Sangeeta Khanna

A Sterling Paperback

STERLING PAPERBACKS
An imprint of
Sterling Publishers (P) Ltd.
A-59, Okhla Industrial Area, Phase-II, New Delhi-110020
Ph. : 26387070, 26386209, Fax : 91-11-26383788
E-mail: ghai@nde.vsnl.net.in

Low Calorie Cooking
©2003, Sterling Publishers (P) Ltd.
ISBN 81 207 2548 4

All rights are reserved. No part of this publication may be reproduced, stored in a retrieval system or transmitted, in any form or by any means, mechanical, photocopying, recording or otherwise, without prior written permission of the publisher.

Published by Sterling Publishers Pvt. Ltd., New Delhi-110020.
Lasertypeset by Vikas Compographics, New Delhi-110020.
Printed at Sai Early Learners Press (P) Ltd.

About the Book

Low Calorie Cooking is sumptuous cooking with an emphasis on health food for figure and weight-conscious people. It offers hearty meals that are comparatively low in fat and calories.

The recipes vary from mouth-watering soups to delicious salads, rice, paneer and other vegetarian dishes. Raitas have also been included, keeping in mind their benefits and nutritive value. These recipes can be made with little oil, retaining the taste of the original. This has been made possible with the help of a variety of seasonings and spices which the Indian style of cooking offers in plenty.

All the servings in this book are for four to five persons.

Throughout the book, an attempt has been made to promote the idea of healthy and nutritious cuisine without compromising on taste. Fresh ingredients, used imaginatively and skilfully, are the focus of this book.

Happy cooking, eating and maintaining your ideal weight!

Weights and Measures

The weights and measures used in this book are in grams and standard weighing cups. One cup measures approximately 200 gm and 1 level teaspoon is equivalent to approximately 5 gm. Similarly, 1 level tablespoon is equivalent to approximately 15 gm or 3 teaspoons.

The oven temperature for baked dishes is usually 200°C, which is equivalent to approximately 400°F or gas mark 6.

Contents

Glossary	6
Soups	10
Salads	23
Rice Delicacies	34
Vegetable and Paneer Delights	45
Raitas	89
Snacks	99

Glossary

Almonds	:	*Badam*		
Aniseed	:	*Saunf*		
Asafoetida	:	*Hing*		
Bay leaf	:	*Tej patta*		
Bengal gram	:	*Chana dal*		
Broccoli	:	*A green vegetable resembling cauliflower*		
Broken wheat	:	*Dalia*		
Brown sugar	:	*Shakkar*		
Capsicum	:	*Shimla mirch*		
Cardamom	:	*Elaichi*		
Cashewnut	:	*Kaju*		
Chickpeas	:	*Kabuli chana*		
Chilli powder	:	*Lal mirch*		
Cinnamon	:	*Dalchini*		
Cloves	:	*Laung*		
Coriander leaves	:	*Hara dhania*		
Coriander seeds	:	*Sukha dhania*		
Corn	:	*Makai*		
Cumin seed	:	*Jeera*		
Dried fenugreek	:	*Kasoori methi*		
Dry coconut	:	*Copra*		
Dry mango powder	:	*Amchoor*		
Fenugreek	:	*Methi*		
Garlic	:	*Lasoon*		
Ginger	:	*Adrak*		
Gram flour	:	*Besan*		
Green chillies	:	*Hari mirch*		
Green peas	:	*Matar*		
Honey	:	*Shahad*		
Lime	:	*Nimbu*		

Mint	:	*Pudina*	*Thymol seeds*	: *Ajwain*
Mustard	:	*Rai*	*Turmeric*	: *Haldi*
Nutmeg	:	*Jaiphal*	*Apple*	: *Seb*
Onion	:	*Pyaz*	*Banana*	: *Kela*
Peppercorn	:	*Kali mirch*	*Black gram*	: *Urad dal*
Pomegranate seeds	:	*Anardana*	*Buttermilk*	: *Chaach*
Poppy seeds	:	*Khus khus*	*Coconut*	: *Nariyal*
Potatoes	:	*Alu*	*Dates*	: *Khajoor*
Raisins	:	*Kishmish*	*Grapes*	: *Angoor*
Red gram	:	*Masoor dal*	*Groundnut*	: *Moongphali*
Refined flour	:	*Maida*	*Guava*	: *Amrood*
Salt	:	*Namak*	*Mango*	: *Aam*
Semolina	:	*Sooji*	*Melon seeds*	: *Magaz*
Spinach	:	*Palak*	*Orange*	: *Narangi*
Split green gram	:	*Moong dhuli dal*	*Pineapple*	: *Ananas*
Tamarind	:	*Imli*	*Pomegranate*	: *Anar*
			Sweet lime	: *Mausambi*

Curry powder or Kitchen King masala	:	*A blend of salt, cumin powder, cinnamon, nutmeg powder, cardamom, peppercorns and artificial flavourings.*
Hung curd	:	*Take required quantity of curd in a muslin cloth. Hang to let the water drain (for about 20 minutes).*
Spring onion stalk	:	*For about 250 gm of spring onions, add 6 cups of water and pressure cook for 5-10 minutes after the first whistle. Cool and strain.*
Vegetable stock	:	*1 cup mixed, sliced vegetables, 6 cups of water, 1 tsp ginger paste, ½ tsp salt, 1 onion, finely chopped. Mix all the ingredients and pressure cook for 5 minutes after the first whistle. Cool and strain to make 5 cups.*

Lentil Soup (pg.10) →

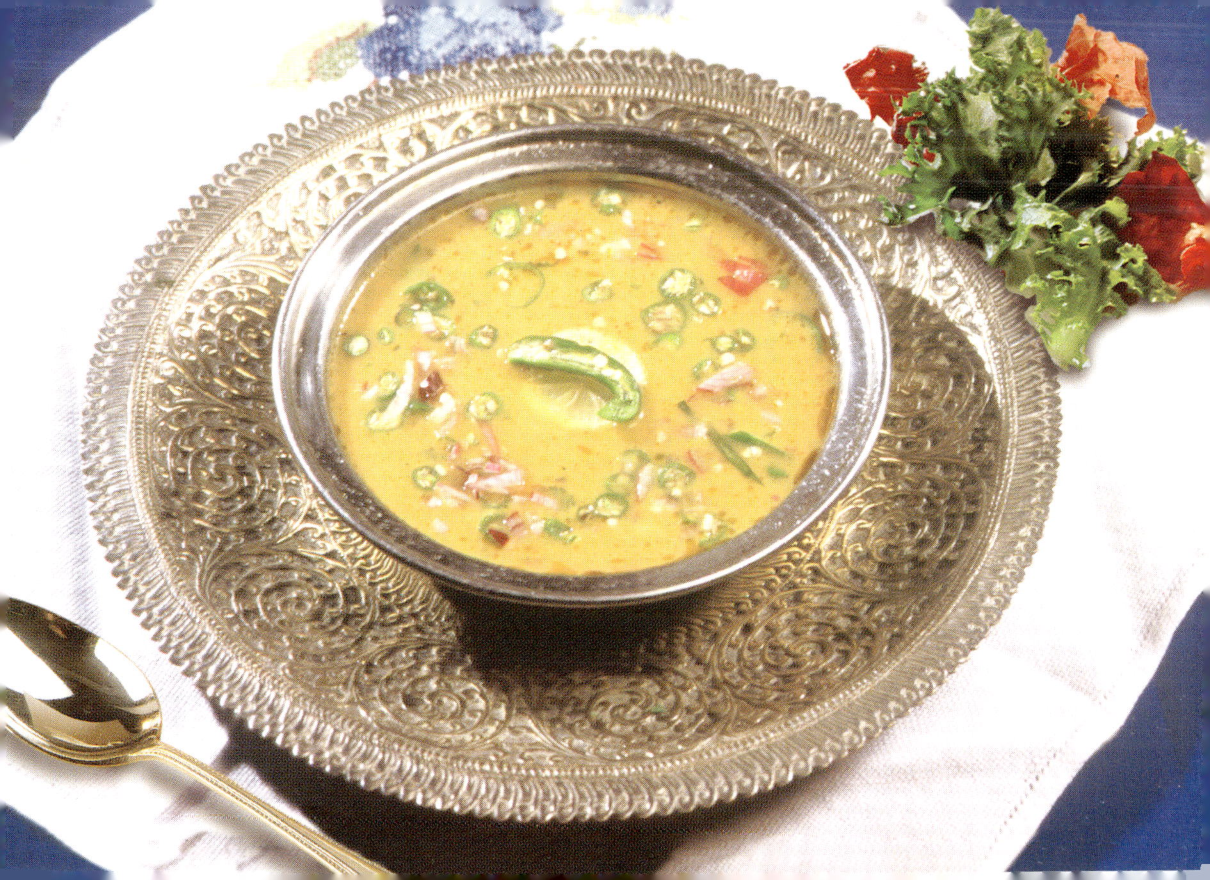

SOUPS

Lentil Soup

Ingredients

1 cup split green gram
½ cup red gram
½ cup finely chopped onions
1 cup finely chopped tomatoes
4 cups water
½ tsp each of ginger paste, turmeric powder and white pepper
1 tsp sugar
Salt to taste

For garnishing

1 or 2 green chillies and 1 onion, roughly chopped
Few slices of lemon

Method

1. Pressure cook the lentil with all the other ingredients in 4 cups water for 5-10 minutes, or till the first whistle. Cook for 5 more minutes after the whistle.
2. Blend in a blender and strain.
3. Heat again. Then pour into individual bowls and sprinkle the white pepper on top.
4. Serve hot garnished with the green chillies, chopped onion and a slice of lemon.

Carrot Soup

Ingredients

1 cup grated carrots
1 cup finely chopped spinach
2 tbsp split green gram
½ cup each of roughly chopped onions, potatoes and tomatoes
1 tbsp margarine
2 tbsp tomato sauce
½ tsp sugar
½ cup chopped coriander leaves
Salt and pepper to taste

Method

1. Wash all the vegetables except the onions and pressure cook in 6 cups of water with the lentil. Cook for 5 minutes after the whistle.
2. Cool, blend in a liquidiser. Reserve the stock.
3. Melt the margarine in a saucepan and saute the onions lightly.
4. Then add the stock, sugar, tomato sauce and salt and pepper.
5. Boil for 5 minutes and garnish with the chopped coriander leaves.
6. Serve hot.

Vegetable Soup

Ingredients

3 tomatoes, finely chopped
1½ tbsp finely chopped cabbage
1½ tbsp each of finely chopped capsicum and cauliflower
1½ tbsp finely chopped onion
1 tsp finely chopped green chillies
1 bay leaf
2 tsp oil
Salt and pepper to taste

Method

1. Heat the oil in a pan and fry the onion till light brown.
2. Add all the vegetables and bay leaf and stir-fry.
3. Then add 3 cups of water and bring it to the boil.
4. Lower the flame, cover and let it simmer for 5-10 minutes.
5. Add salt and pepper. Remove the bay leaf and serve hot.

Mushroom Soup

Ingredients

100 gm fresh button mushrooms, finely chopped
½ medium-sized onion, finely chopped
1 tsp butter, 3½ cups water
Salt and pepper to taste

Method

1. Heat the butter in a pan and saute the mushrooms and onion for 2 minutes. Add 3 or 3½ cups water and cook. When tender, remove from the fire.

2. Let it cool and then blend in a blender and strain. Add salt and pepper. Reheat and serve hot.

Spinach Soup

Ingredients

5 cups water
2 seasoning cubes
4 cups finely chopped spinach
¼ cup finely chopped onion
½ tsp each of ginger and garlic paste
1 tsp skimmed milk
1 cup buttermilk, 2 tbsp oil
2 tbsp grated cheese
¼ cup tomato puree
½ tsp pepper powder
Salt to taste

Method

1. Boil together the spinach, seasoning cubes and water for 10 minutes. Remove from the fire.
2. Heat the oil in a saucepan, add the onion and ginger and garlic pastes. Saute for 2 minutes.
3. Then add the tomato puree and boiled spinach. Boil together for 5 minutes.
4. Cool the mixture and blend in a blender till smooth.
5. Transfer the spinach puree into a pot and heat again, adding the milk and buttermilk.
6. Cook for 5 minutes.
7. Serve in soup bowls with the grated cheese sprinkled on top.

Spinach Soup (pg.17) →

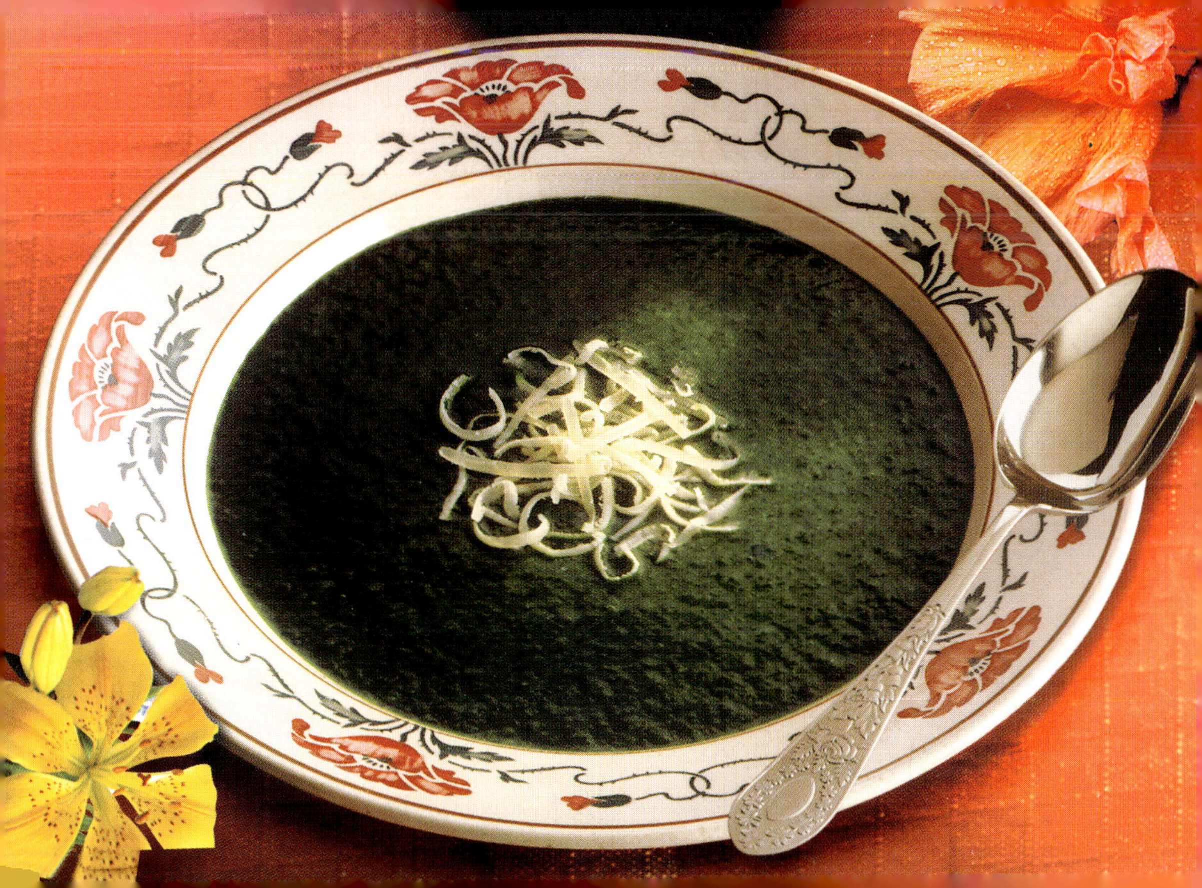

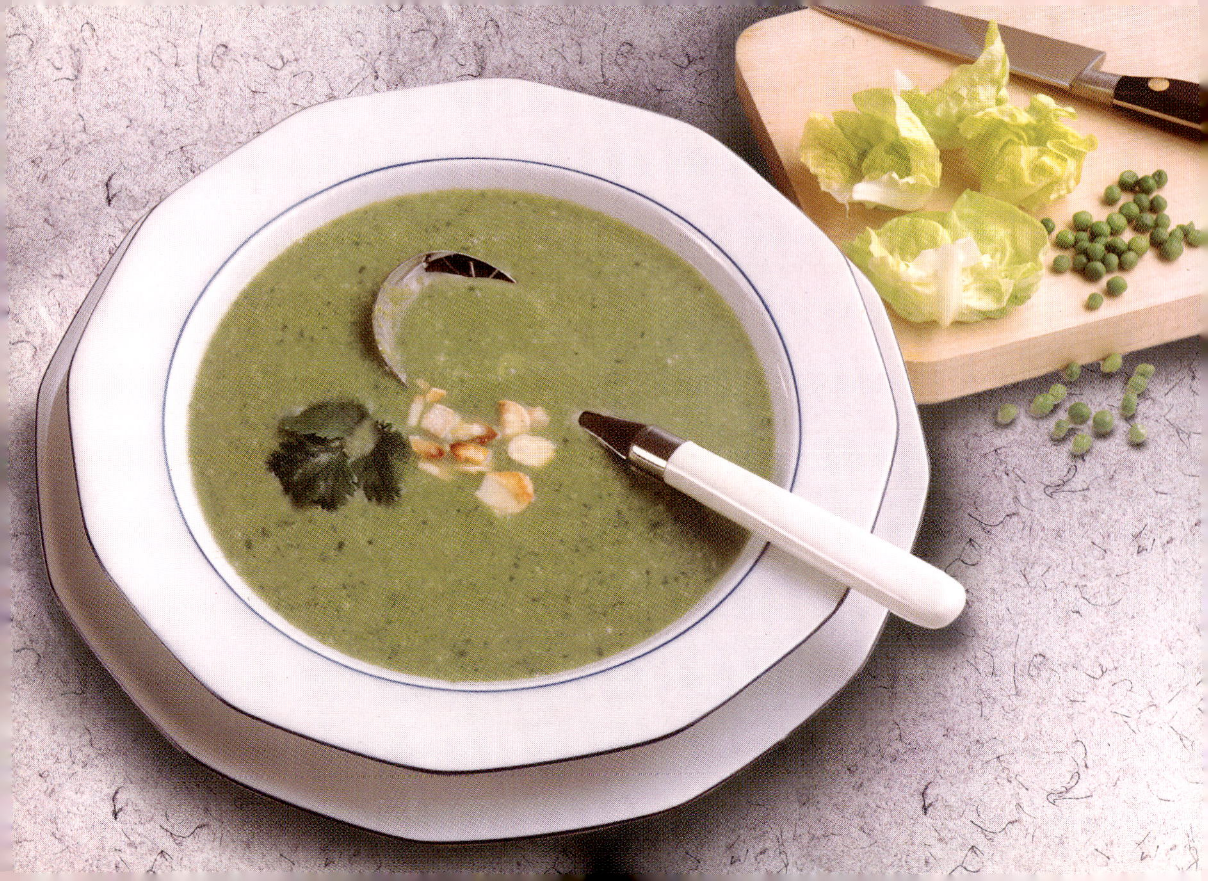

Paneer Pea Soup

Ingredients

½ l milk
2 tbsp lime juice or ¼ tsp citric acid
100 gm shelled peas
1 tbsp finely chopped coriander leaves
1½ + ¼ cups water
Mint sprigs and blanched almonds for garnishing
Salt & pepper to taste

←

How to make cottage cheese

Heat the milk to the boiling stage and add 2 teaspoons of lime juice, or ¼ teaspoon of citric acid dissolved in ¼ cup water. Stir continuously till the clear whey separates. When the coagulum separates from the whey, press to remove all moisture. Keep it aside and reserve 2½ cups of whey.

Method

1. Boil the peas and grind into a paste. Then blend the cottage cheese into a paste.
2. Boil 1½ cups of water and pour the whey into it.
3. Add the pea and cottage cheese pastes to it.
4. Boil for 5 -10 minutes and then add salt and pepper. Mix well.
5. Add the remaining lime juice and coriander leaves.
6. Serve hot garnished with the mint sprigs and almonds.

SALADS

Sprouts Salad

Ingredients

1 cup sprouted green gram
½ cup sprouted black chickpeas
½ cup finely chopped onion
1 cup finely chopped tomatoes
1 tbsp freshly grated coconut
2 tbsp lime juice, 1 tbsp honey
1 tsp pepper powder
Salt to taste

Method

1. Mix all the ingredients and toss well.
2. Chill and serve.

Mixed Vegetable Salad

Ingredients

1 cup carrot, thinly sliced
1 cup finely chopped capsicum
1 cup finely chopped broccoli
½ cup finely chopped cabbage
½ cup spring onion stalk
2 tbsp roasted crushed peanuts
4 cups hot water
1 tsp salt

For the dressing

2 tbsp oil
½ tsp mustard sauce
1 tsp cumin powder
2 tbsp lime juice
1 tbsp cumin seeds
¼ tsp thymol
1 tsp white pepper powder
2 tbsp coriander leaves
A pinch of sugar
Salt to taste

Method

1. Wash all the vegetables thoroughly and drain.
2. Boil the water and add 1 teaspoon salt to it. Soak the vegetables in salted water for 10 minutes.
3. Drain off the water and keep the vegetables aside.
4. Heat the oil, add the cumin seeds to it.
5. Remove from the fire, cool and add rest of the ingredients for the dressing to it.
6. Place the vegetables in a greased baking dish and bake in a hot oven at 200°C for 5 minutes.
7. Remove from the baking tray, mix with the dressing.
8. Then sprinkle the crushed peanuts on it and serve.

Green Fruit Salad

Ingredients

2 green apples
Juice of 2 limes
1 medium-sized, ripe avocado
4 kiwi fruits
1 cup seedless green grapes, trimmed
Mint sprigs for garnishing

For the dressing

4 tbsp ginger wine
2 pieces stem ginger in syrup, drained and sliced

Method

1. Core the apples, then cut into halves and slice thinly, lengthwise. Toss the apples in half of the lime juice and keep aside.
2. Cut the avocado in half lengthwise, then discard the stone and peel. Slice the avocado flesh lengthwise. Toss the slices in the remaining lime juice and keep aside.
3. Peel the kiwi fruits. Cut lengthwise into quarters and place in the serving bowl.
4. Drain the apples and avocado, add to the serving bowl with the grapes, ginger wine and ginger. Mix gently. Garnish with the mint and serve.

Note: Dressing should be added only at the time of serving.

Greet Fruit Salad (pg.27) →

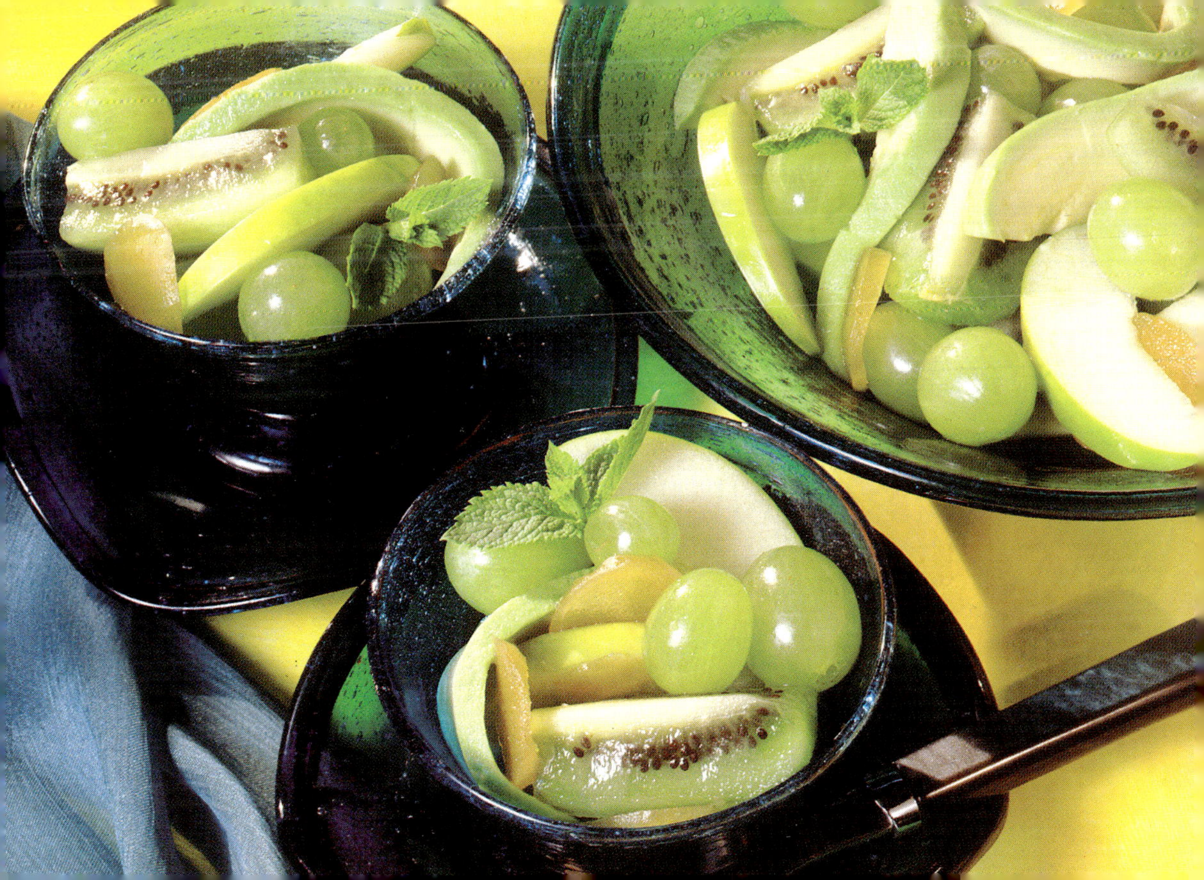

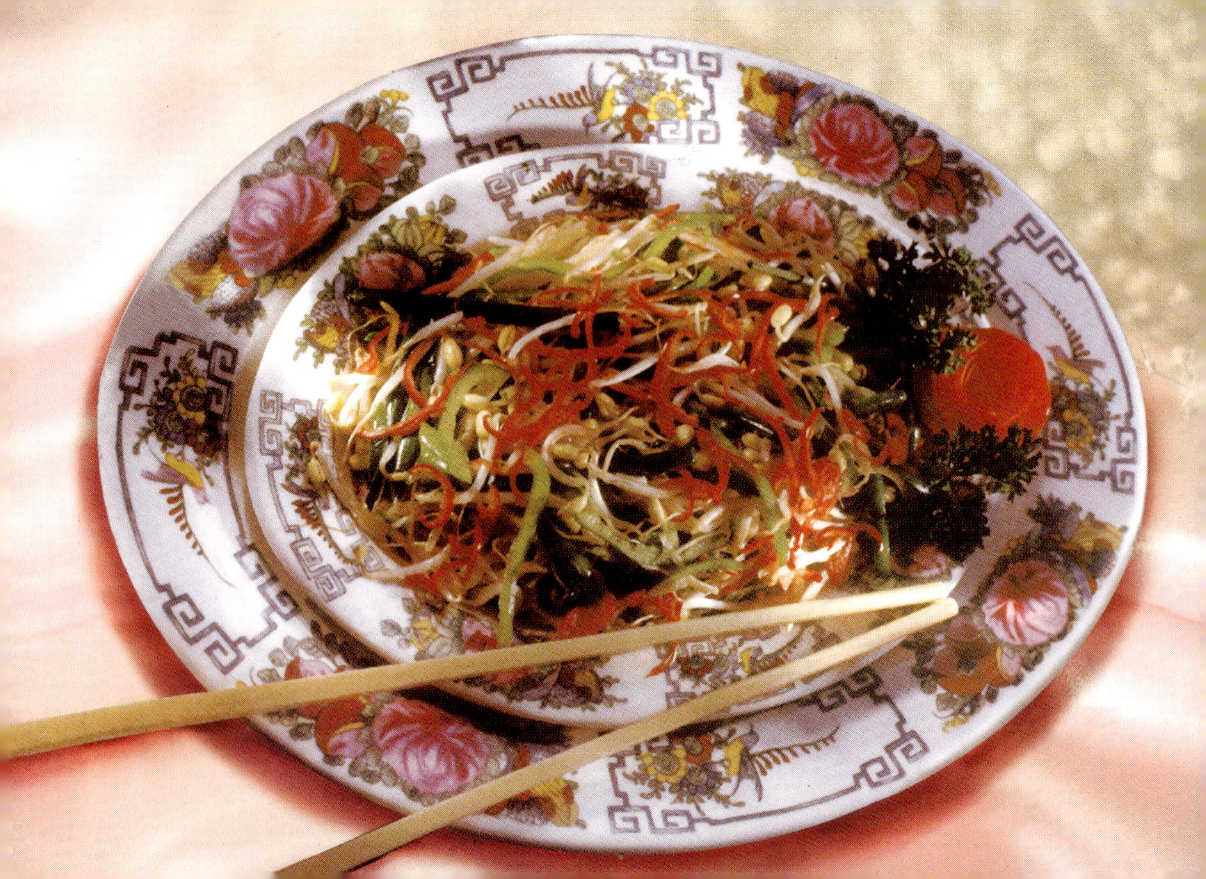

Tossed Salad

Ingredients

1 capsicum
1 large tomato
1 onion
1 radish
2 cucumbers
1 carrot
¼ cup cheese cubes or cottage cheese
½ cup boiled peas
½ cup bean sprouts

←

For the dressing

4 tbsp tomato sauce
2 tbsp oil
3 tbsp vinegar
1/3 tsp mustard powder
½ tsp sugar
Salt and pepper to taste

Method

1. Cut the vegetables into desired shapes.
2. Mix the ingredients for the dressing in a glass bottle. Shake the bottle till it mixes well.
3. Toss the salad in the dressing and serve immediately.

Paneer Sprouts Salad

Ingredients

1 cup chopped cottage cheese
1 cup each of green gram and wheat sprouts
3 tbsp grated coconut
1 tbsp honey
2 tbsp lime juice
1 tbsp chopped coriander leaves
Salt and pepper to taste

Method

1. Mix well all the ingredients except the coconut.
2. Then garnish with the grated coconut and serve immediately.

RICE DELICACIES

Carrot Khichadi

Ingredients

1 cup rice
½ cup split green gram
1½ cups grated carrot
½ cup finely chopped onion
1 tsp each of ginger and green chilli paste
½ cup coriander leaves
2 tbsp oil, 3 cups water
½ tsp turmeric powder
Whole garam masala (1 stick cinnamon, 2 cloves, 1 cardamom)
2 bay leaves
Salt to taste

Method

1. Wash the rice and lentil properly. Mix the two.
2. Add the grated carrot to it and keep aside.
3. Heat the oil. Fry the whole *garam masala* (cardamom, cloves and cinnamon) and bay leaves for a few seconds.
4. Add the onion and fry till light brown.
5. Add the ginger and green chilli pastes.
6. Then add the water and the rice, lentil and carrot mixture with the turmeric powder and salt.
7. Pressure cook for 5 minutes after the whistle.
8. Add the coriander leaves and serve hot.

Chana Pulao

Ingredients

1 cup rice
1 cup chickpeas
½ cup curd
¼ cup milk
2 tbsp oil
2 tbsp chopped coriander leaves
Whole garam masala (1 stick cinnamon, 2 cloves, 2 cardamoms)
Salt and pepper to taste

Method

1. Wash the rice properly. Then boil it in 2½ cups water with the whole *garam masala* till the rice is tender. Drain and keep aside.
2. Soak the chickpeas overnight. Pressure cook in 4 cups water with salt. Cook for 20 minutes after the whistle. Let the pressure drop by itself so that the water dries up completely.
3. Dilute the curd with ¼ cup milk and mix well.
4. In a greased pan arrange a layer of rice. Pour half the curd on top of the rice. Then arrange one part of the chickpeas on top of it.
5. Repeat the layers till all is consumed. Sprinkle the coriander leaves and cover with foil.
6. Bake in a preheated oven at 200°C for 10 minutes.
7. Serve hot.

Spicy Corn Pulao

Ingredients

1 cup washed rice
1 cup cooked corn or tinned corn
1 cup each of finely chopped capsicums and tomatoes
1 cup thinly sliced onions
2 tbsp each of green chilli-ginger paste and coconut paste
½ cup roughly chopped coriander leaves
4 cups water
2 tbsp coriander-cumin powder
1 tsp chilli powder
2 tbsp oil
Salt to taste

→

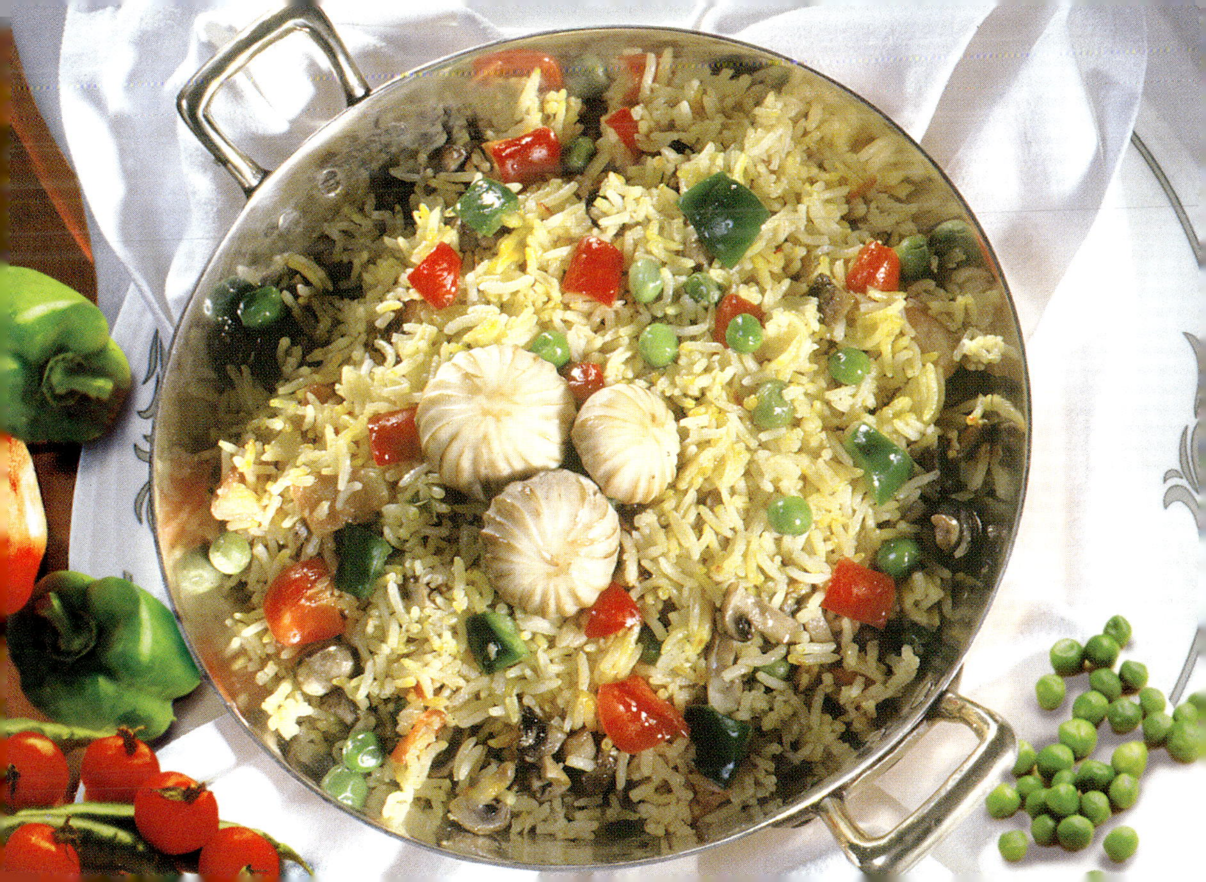

Method

1. Wash the rice properly and keep aside.
2. In a heavy-duty pan heat the oil. Fry the onions and ginger-chilli paste in it till the paste is brown in colour.
3. Add the tomatoes, corn, capsicums, coconut paste and all the dry *masalas*. Cook for 2 minutes.
4. Boil the water in a separate container and then add the water, washed rice, coriander leaves and salt in the pan. Cook till done.
5. Serve hot.

Broken Wheat Khichadi

Ingredients

1 cup rice
½ cup broken wheat
½ cup curd
2½ cups water
½ cup finely chopped onions
½ cup boiled peas
½ cup finely chopped and boiled carrots
1 tsp chilli-garlic paste
2 tsp oil
½ cup grated coconut
Salt to taste

Method

1. In a pressure cooker pour 1 teaspoon oil and fry the wheat for 5 minutes.
2. Add the rice to it and mix well.
3. Mix the water and curd in a bowl and then add to the rice and wheat mixture. Add salt.
4. Pressure cook for 5 minutes after the whistle.
5. Pour 1 teaspoon oil in a saucepan, add the chopped onions, chilli-garlic paste, boiled vegetables and coconut. Cook for 5 minutes. Then add salt and cook for 5-10 minutes.
6. Pour the vegetable mixture over the cooked rice and broken wheat. Mix well and serve hot.

Coconut Kheer

Ingredients

1 cup grated coconut
¼ cup rice
¼ cup sugar
2 tbsp honey
½ tsp cardamom powder
A few nuts (optional)

Method

1. Extract the coconut milk by adding 3 cups of warm water to the grated coconut. Strain and reserve 2½ cups of it.
2. Boil the rice in water till cooked. Drain off the water. Blend well in a blender.
3. Then heat the coconut milk in a large saucepan over a low flame.
4. Add the blended rice to it along with the sugar and cardamom powder.
5. Add the honey when the mixture thickens. Add the nuts.
6. Cool and serve.

VEGETABLE AND PANEER DELIGHTS

Chinese Vegetables in Vinegar

Ingredients

1½ cups mixed diced vegetables (carrot, capsicum, cabbage, beans)
½ cup vinegar
1 tbsp garlic paste
1 tbsp oil
¼ tsp sugar
1 tbsp cornflour
½ cup water
2 tsp soya sauce
1 tbsp tomato sauce
1 tsp pepper powder
Salt to taste

Method

1. Dissolve the cornflour in water to form a smooth paste.
2. Then mix the rest of the ingredients in the cornflour paste. Marinate the vegetables in this paste for half an hour.
3. Then pressure cook the vegetables till the first whistle.
4. Add the dissolved cornflour to it.
5. Continue stirring till a thick consistency is obtained.
6. Serve hot.

Full Protein Roti

Ingredients

1 cup each of wheat flour and gram flour
¼ cup soyabean flour
½ cup each of grated carrot and curd
½ cup sprouted green gram
2 tbsp finely chopped spring onions
1 tbsp grated onion
1 tbsp chopped green chillies
½ cup thymol seeds
¼ cup grated coconut
2 tbsp oil, ½ cup curd
Salt and pepper to taste

Method

1. Roast the wheat, soyabean and gram flour for 5 minutes, stirring continuously.
2. Cool and add salt.
3. Knead into a soft dough with the curd (the curd should not be cold). Keep aside for half an hour.
4. For the stuffing, squeeze out the water from the grated onion.
5. Then mix all the remaining ingredients with the onion.
6. Take a small portion of the dough and form into a ball.
7. Flatten the ball slightly and fill it with 2 tablespoons of the filling.

Full Protein Roti (pg.47) →

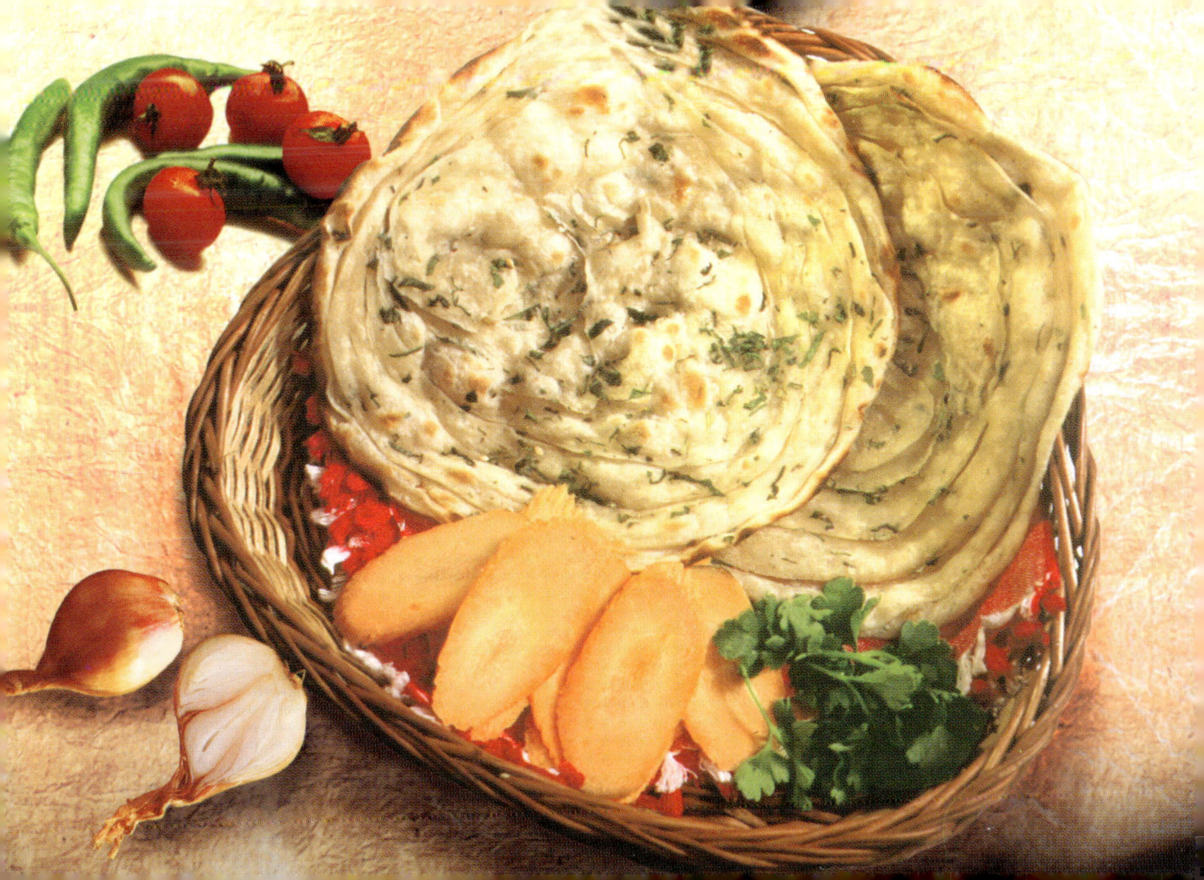

8. Then close it, keeping the filling in the centre.
9. Roll it out, dusted with the flour, into a chapati.
10. Cook the chapati on a hot griddle on a medium flame till brown.
11. Repeat the same with the remaining balls and stuffing.
12. Serve hot as an accompaniment to any of the vegetable or cottage cheese dishes, applying a little butter before serving.

Pickled Vegetables

Ingredients

*1 cup mixed vegetables
(carrot, cabbage, capsicum)
½ cup spring onion stalk
1 tsp each of ginger and garlic paste
2 tbsp coriander leaves
2 tbsp lime juice
1 tsp each of cumin and coriander powder
½ tsp freshly ground mustard powder
½ tsp brown sugar
Green chillies and salt to taste*

Method

1. Cut all the vegetables into slices or large chunks.
2. Steam them for 5 minutes.
3. Drain off the water and leave them on a strainer to cool.
4. When cool, put the vegetables into a bowl, add all the *masalas* and mix well.
5. Chill and serve.

Mixed Vegetable Pickle

Ingredients

2 cups mixed vegetables
¼ cup lime juice
1 tbsp chilli powder
1 tbsp mustard powder
½ tsp asafoetida
½ cup gingelly oil
1 tsp salt

Method

1. Cut the vegetables into thin strips.
2. Wash properly and pat dry.
3. Add the lime juice, mustard, salt, chilli powder and asafoetida. Mix well.
4. Pour the gingelly oil over it. Lightly mix and keep aside for two days before use.

Dahi Alu Masala

Ingredients

8-10 small, round potatoes
1 cup curd (prepared out of skimmed milk)
½ cup finely chopped onions
1 tsp each of ginger and garlic paste
1 tbsp oil
1 tbsp coriander powder
1 tsp each of garam masala, chilli powder and whole cumin seeds
½ tsp mustard seeds
1 tbsp ground pomegranate seeds
Few coriander leaves for garnishing
Salt to taste

Method

1. Boil the potatoes. Let them cool. Then peel and keep aside.
2. Heat the oil. Fry the mustard seeds.
3. Add the chopped onions and saute till they are transparent.
4. Then add the ginger and garlic pastes. Cook for 2 minutes.
5. Add the peeled potatoes, salt and all the dry *masalas*.
6. Add the ground pomegranate seeds and curd and stir-fry till the potatoes are evenly coated with the curd mixture.
7. Sprinkle the coriander leaves over it and serve hot.

Green Peas and Tomato Masala

Ingredients

2½ cups shelled green peas
½ cup finely chopped onions
1 cup finely chopped tomatoes
1 tbsp each of ginger and garlic paste
1 tbsp lime juice
1 tbsp oil
1 tsp each of garam masala, chilli powder,
pepper and turmeric powder
Salt to taste

Method

1. Boil the green peas in 2 cups of water and keep aside.
2. Pour the oil in a heavy-duty pan. Fry the chopped onions, ginger and garlic till they are transparent.
3. Add the boiled green peas, keeping aside the stock, and the dry *masalas* and cook for 5 minutes.
4. Then add salt and the pea stock. Cook till the stock dries up.
5. Stir in the tomatoes and lime juice.
6. Cook for 5 minutes and remove from the fire.
7. Serve hot with rice or any bread.

Baby Corn Curry

Ingredients

200 gm baby corns
½ cup chopped onion
1 tsp chopped garlic
½ cup each of coriander and mint leaves
1 tsp chopped green chillies
2 tbsp oil
2 cups coconut milk
½ cup tomato puree
1 tsp garam masala powder
1 tbsp poppy seeds
Salt and pepper to taste

Method

1. Pressure cook the baby corns in 1½ cups salted water till the first whistle. When slightly cool, slice them into halves.
2. Grind the onion, garlic, mint, coriander leaves, green chillies and poppy seeds together into a paste.
3. Heat the oil, fry the paste till the mixture leaves the oil.
4. Add the tomato puree and dry *masalas* and cook for 2 minutes.
5. Then add salt and the boiled baby corn pieces. Fry for 5 minutes.
6. Finally, add the coconut milk and simmer till a thick gravy consistency is obtained.
7. Serve hot.

Sweet and Sour Vegetables

Ingredients

¼ cup roughly chopped capsicums
½ cup each of roughly chopped cucumber and tomatoes
2 cups vegetable stock
2½ tbsp cornflour
½ cup each of water and vinegar
¼ tsp each of ajinomoto and white pepper
⅓ cup sugar
Salt to taste

Method

1. Mix the water with the cornflour and keep aside.
2. In a saucepan, pour the vinegar and then add the sugar and vegetable stock, ajinomoto, white pepper and salt. Cook for 10 minutes.
3. Then add the chopped vegetables and cornflour and cook till it thickens.
4. Serve hot.

Spicy Potatoes

Ingredients

½ kg small potatoes
¼ cup mint chutney
½ cup curd
1 tbsp oil
½ tsp mustard seeds
1 tbsp crushed pomegranate seeds
½ tsp pepper
Salt to taste

Method

1. Boil the potatoes. Peel and prick with a fork and apply the mint chutney over them.
2. Heat the oil. Fry the mustard seeds. When they splutter, add the potatoes. Saute for a minute.
3. Add the curd, pepper and salt. Mix well. Cook till the curd dries up completely and the chutney coats the potatoes.
4. Serve with the crushed pomegranate seeds sprinkled on top.

Peas Corn Masala

Ingredients

250 gm boiled peas
1 cup fresh boiled corn or tinned corn
½ cup onion paste
1 tsp each of ginger, garlic and green chilli paste
2 tbsp coriander leaves paste
2 tbsp coconut paste
2 tbsp oil
1 tsp each of cashewnut, poppy seed and melon seed paste
1 tsp each of garam masala and dried fenugreek
Salt to taste

Method

1. Pressure cook the peas and fresh corn together in 2 cups of water. (Do not boil the tinned corn.)
2. Dry the water completely.
3. Heat the oil. Fry the onion paste till light brown in colour.
4. Add the ginger and garlic pastes to it. Fry for another 2 minutes.
5. Add the poppy seed, cashewnut and melon seed pastes and the coconut, coriander leaves and green chilli pastes. Cook for 5 minutes.
6. Add the peas and corn and fry for 5 minutes, adding half a cup of water.
7. Add salt and the *garam masala* and dried fenugreek. Remove from the fire and serve hot.

Paneer Tawa Masala

Ingredients

250 gm cottage cheese
1½ cups finely chopped onions
1 tsp ginger, roughly chopped
4 green chillies, roughly chopped
½ tsp finely chopped coriander leaves
4 tbsp oil
1 tsp thymol seeds
½ tsp each of chilli and coriander powder
½ tsp each of garam masala and chat masala

For the gravy

5 tomatoes
½ cup ginger paste
½ tsp garlic paste
2 green chillies, roughly chopped
½ tsp chilli powder
1 tsp dried fenugreek
2 cloves
1 cardamom
Salt to taste

Paneer Tawa Masala (pg.67) →

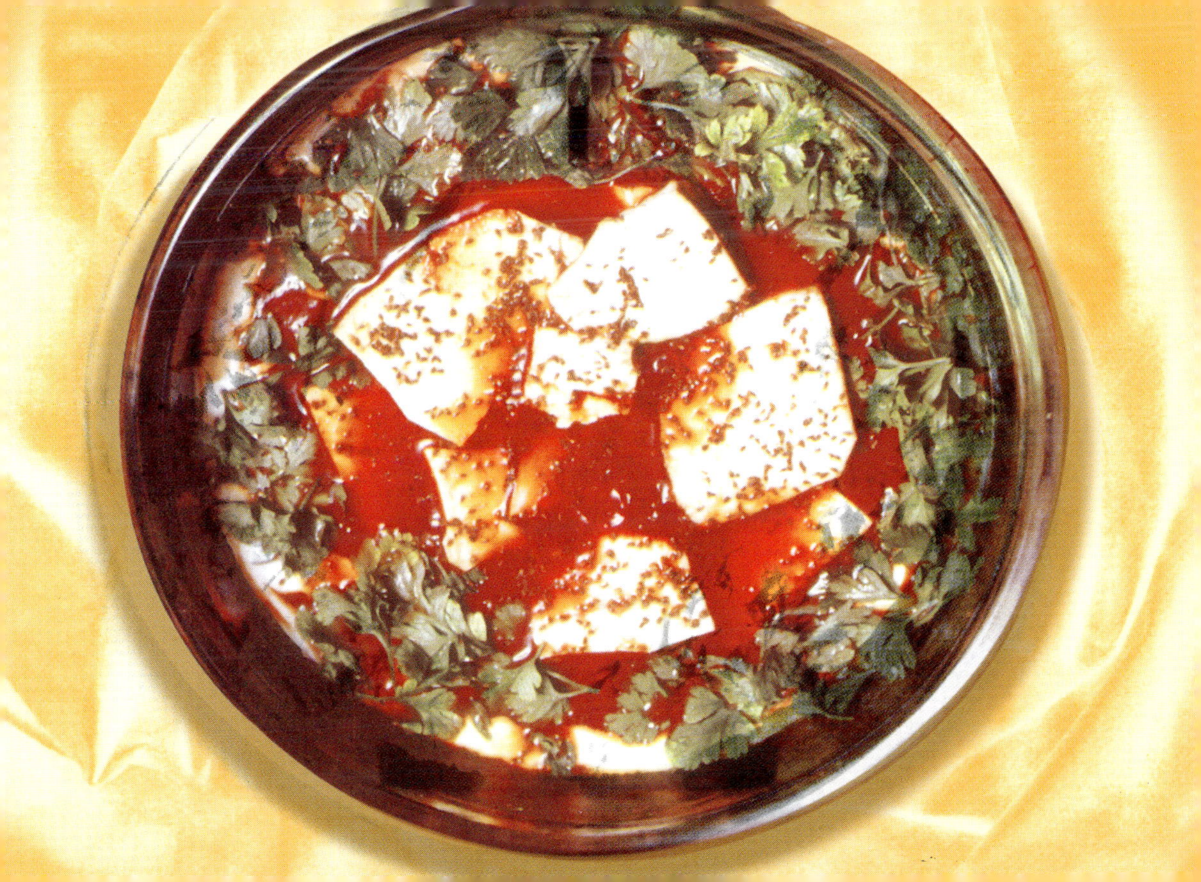

Method

1. Blend the tomatoes with ¼ cup water in a blender. Strain and reserve the puree.
2. In a saucepan, pour the puree and add the ginger and garlic pastes to it, along with the green chillies, chilli powder, cardamom and cloves. Cook on a low flame, slowly bringing it to the boil until it thickens slightly.
3. Then add the dried fenugreek and keep aside.
4. Cut the cottage cheese into about 1" cubes.
5. Heat the oil on a griddle and saute the thymol on a medium flame.
6. Add the chopped onions, ginger and green chillies. Saute till the onions turn transparent. Then add the chilli powder, coriander powder, *chat masala* and gravy.
7. Add the cottage cheese cubes to this. Cook till the gravy coats the pieces. Add the *garam masala* and coriander leaves and serve hot.

Chana Soya Delight

Ingredients

½ cup chickpeas
¼ cup soya nuggets
½ cup finely chopped onions
½ cup finely chopped tomatoes
1 tsp ginger paste
1 tsp green chilli paste
1 tsp oil
1 tsp crushed pomegranate seeds
1 tsp cumin powder
1 tsp chat masala
Salt to taste

Method

1. Soak the chickpeas overnight in 2 cups of water.
2. Pressure cook in the same water for 20 minutes on a medium flame, till they are cooked.
3. Soak the nuggets in water for an hour. Then drain and keep aside.
4. Heat the oil, fry the chopped onions till they turn transparent.
5. Add the ginger paste and fry for 2 minutes. Add the green chilli paste.
6. Then add the tomatoes and cook till they are tender.
7. Add the soya nuggets and boiled chickpeas. Finally add all the dry *masalas* and salt.
8. Stir for a minute and serve hot.

Mixed Lentils

Ingredients

¼ cup each of red gram, split green gram, Bengal gram and black gram
2 cups roughly chopped spinach
½ cup roughly chopped coriander leaves
1 cup thinly sliced onions
1 tsp chopped green chillies
1 cup grated ginger
1 cup finely chopped tomatoes
1 tbsp oil
1 tsp each of turmeric, coriander, cumin and garam masala powder
Salt to taste

Method

1. Clean and wash all the lentils. Pressure cook in 3½ cups water with the turmeric powder, washed spinach and salt. Cook for 5 minutes after the whistle.
2. Heat the oil. Fry the onions till light brown in colour. Add the ginger, tomatoes and all the dry *masalas*.
3. Add the green chillies and coriander leaves.
4. Add the lentils to the above mixture. Cook till the required thickness is reached.
5. Serve hot.

Chana Masala

Ingredients

1 cup chickpeas
1 cup thinly sliced onions
1" piece ginger
2 chopped green chillies
1 tbsp lime juice/tamarind juice
2 tbsp chopped coriander leaves
1 tsp pomegranate seeds
1 tsp each of cumin powder, chilli powder,
Chat masala and black salt
1 tbsp dried mango powder
1 tsp Kitchen King masala or curry powder
Salt to taste

Method

1. Soak the chickpeas overnight.
2. Pressure cook the chickpeas in 4 cups water with salt for 20 minutes after the whistle. Then simmer till the water dries completely.
3. Cool to room temperature.
4. Grind the pomegranate seeds and keep aside.
5. Add all the dry *masalas* to the chickpeas.
6. Saute the onions in 1 teaspoon oil to a transparent stage. Add to the chickpeas.
7. Sprinkle the green chillies, lime juice (or tamarind juice) and coriander leaves.
8. Serve hot or cold.

Vegetable Barbeque

Ingredients

200 gm cottage cheese, cut into chunks
1 each of capsicum, tomato and onion
1 cup curd
1 tsp each of ginger and garlic paste
1 tsp oil
A pinch of tandoori colour
1 tsp each of garam masala powder and chat masala
Juice of 2 limes
Salt to taste

Method

1. Hang the curd in a muslin cloth and let the water drain.
2. In a bowl, place the curd and add the ginger and garlic pastes, oil, tandoori colour, *garam masala*, *chat masala* and salt to it. Mix well.
3. Cut the capsicum and onion into big pieces and add to the curd mixture. Cut the tomato into big pieces, remove the seeds and then add to the mixture.
4. Take the cottage cheese chunks and add to the curd mixture. Mix well and keep aside for ½ an hour.
5. Take a skewer and insert one capsicum piece. Follow it up with a tomato and an onion piece. Then insert a cottage cheese piece. Repeat till the skewer is full, leaving 1" on both sides.
6. Grill or bake in a tandoor for 5 to 10 minutes.
7. Squeeze the lime juice over them and serve hot.

Spicy Paneer Peas Masala

Ingredients

200 gm cottage cheese, cut into cubes
1 cup boiled peas
1 onion, finely chopped
2 tbsp each of mint leaves, coriander leaves and green chilli-garlic paste
¼ cup coconut paste
1 tbsp lime juice
1 tsp garam masala
½ tsp cumin powder
2 tbsp oil
2 tbsp curd
Salt to taste

Method

1. Pour the oil in a saucepan and fry the onions till they are transparent.
2. Add the pastes and lime juice.
3. Add the peas and saute for 5 minutes.
4. Then add the cottage cheese, cumin powder, *garam masala* and salt.
5. Add the curd, mix well and cook for a few minutes on a low flame.
6. Serve hot.

Chilli Paneer

Ingredients

1 cup cottage cheese chunks
1 tsp garlic paste
1 tbsp green chilli paste
1 tbsp oil
2 tbsp tomato sauce
½ cup water
1 tbsp soya sauce
2 tbsp vinegar
¼ tsp ajinomoto (optional)
A pinch of tandoori colour (orange-red)
Salt to taste

Method

1. Mix all the ingredients except the oil. Cook till the water has dried completely.
2. Add the oil. Toss till the cottage cheese is well coated with the sauces.
3. Mix well and serve hot.

Pudina Paneer

Ingredients

200 gm cottage cheese, cut into cubes
1 cup finely chopped mint leaves
½ cup finely chopped coriander leaves
½ cup onion paste
½ cup curd
1 tbsp each of oil and lime juice
2-3 green chillies, slit into halves
1 tsp each of cumin seeds and sugar
1 tbsp pomegranate seeds
1 tbsp chilli powder
Salt to taste

Method

1. Grind all the ingredients together except the cottage cheese, oil, curd, chilli powder and salt.
2. Marinate the cottage cheese pieces in the ground paste. Keep aside for an hour.
3. Then cook for 5 minutes on a medium flame and remove from the fire. Add the oil, curd, salt and chilli powder.
4. Cook for 5 more minutes. Serve hot.

Paneer Spinach Delight

Ingredients

3 cups finely chopped spinach
1 cup diced cottage cheese
1 cup bean sprouts
½ cup pineapple bits
2 cups water
1 tsp soya sauce
1 tbsp each of vinegar, oil, tomato sauce and garlic paste
½ tsp white pepper
A pinch of ajinomoto
Salt to taste

Method

1. Pour the water in a saucepan and bring it to the boil. Remove from the fire.
2. Add the spinach and bean sprouts to it. Soak in the water for a minute and then drain.
3. Heat the oil, add the garlic to it and fry for a minute.
4. Add the spinach, bean sprouts, cottage cheese and pineapple bits to it. Stir-fry for 2 minutes.
5. Add the soya sauce, vinegar, tomato sauce, pepper, ajinomoto and salt.
6. Serve hot.

Palak Paneer

Ingredients

5 cups coarsely chopped spinach, stems removed
200 gm cottage cheese, cut into thick squares
½ cup finely chopped onions
1 tomato, finely chopped
1 tsp each of ginger and garlic paste
1 cup milk
4 green chillies, slit into halves
1 tbsp oil
1 tsp each of garam masala, chat masala and chilli powder
Salt to taste

Method

1. Pressure cook the spinach in 1 cup water till the first whistle. Let it cool.
2. Then grind it in a grinder to a fine paste.
3. Heat the oil. Fry the chopped onions, ginger and garlic.
4. Add the chopped tomatoes and cook till they are tender.
5. Add the green chillies.
6. Then add the spinach to the mixture and all the dry *masalas*, with salt. Cook for 15 minutes.
7. Add the cottage cheese pieces to the spinach.
8. Add the milk and cook till the required consistency is reached.
9. Serve hot.

RAITAS

Pineapple Raita

Ingredients

1 cup chopped fresh pineapple
2½ cups curd (prepared out of skimmed milk)
1 tbsp honey
1 tsp sugar
½ cup water
A pinch of cardamom powder

Method

1. Cook the chopped pineapple in the water with the sugar till tender. Cool and keep aside.

2. Strain the curd. Add the cooked pineapple pieces, honey and cardamom powder to it. Chill and serve.

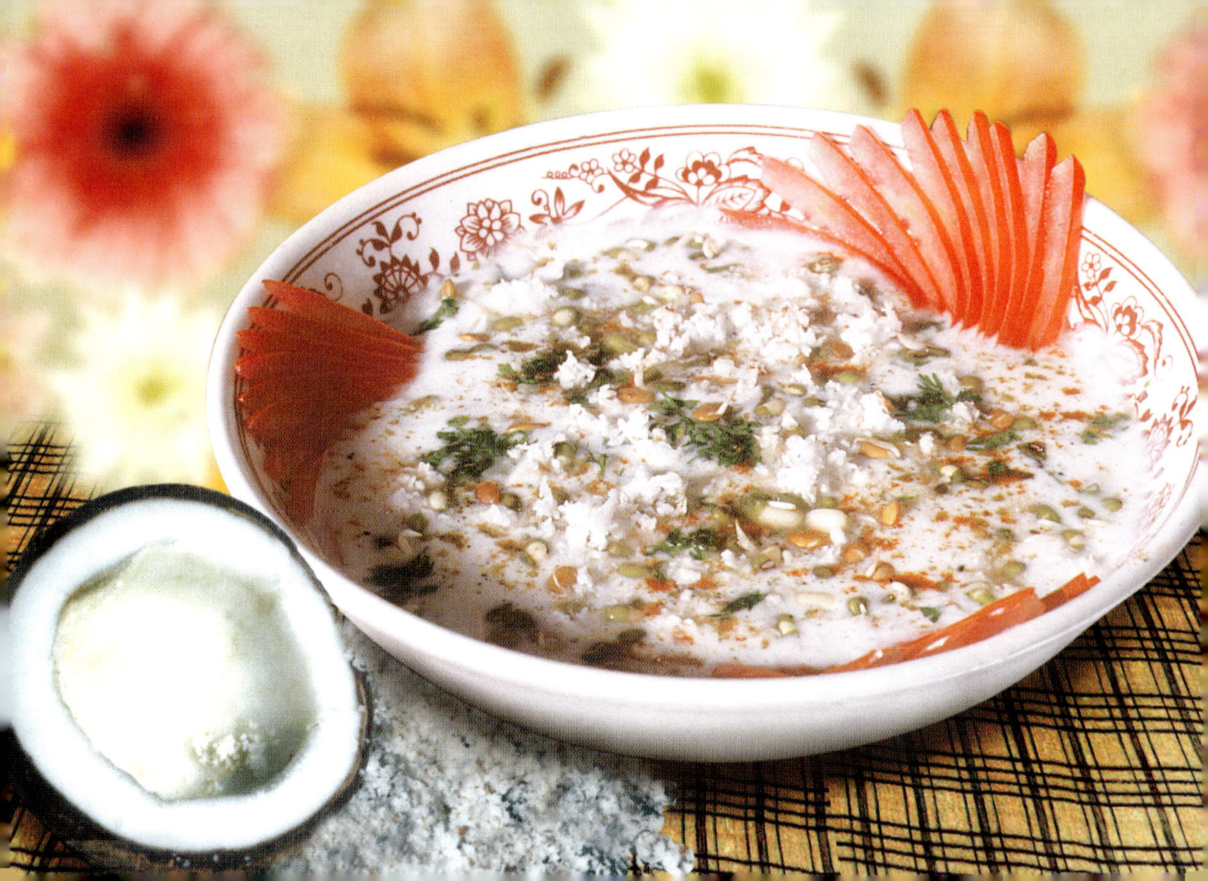

Coconut Raita

Ingredients

½ cup fresh grated coconut
2 cups curd (prepared out of skimmed milk)
1 tbsp each of finely chopped mint leaves and coriander leaves
½ tsp cumin seeds, roasted and coarsely ground
½ tsp pepper powder
Salt to taste

Method

1. Strain the curd. Add all the ingredients to it. Mix well.
2. Serve chilled.

←

Mango Raita

Ingredients

½ cup mango pulp
2 cups curd (made out of skimmed milk)
1 tbsp finely chopped coriander leaves
½ tsp oil, ¼ tsp mustard seeds
⅛ tsp fenugreek seeds
Salt and pepper to taste

Method

1. Strain the curd. Add the mango pulp, salt and pepper.
2. Heat the oil. Fry the mustard and fenugreek seeds. Add to the curd.
3. Then add the coriander and mix well. Serve chilled.

Fruit Raita

Ingredients

1 cup fresh, finely chopped pineapple
½ cup banana slices
2½ cups low fat curd (prepared out of skimmed milk)
1 tbsp finely chopped coriander leaves
1 tbsp sugar, ½ cup water
1 tbsp lime juice
1 tsp cumin powder
1 tsp dried mint leaves, powdered
½ tsp pepper powder
½ tsp pomegranate seeds
Salt to taste

Method

1. Cook the pineapple in the water till tender. Add the lime juice and sugar to it.
2. Add the banana slices and let it cool.
3. Strain the curd.
4. Add the cumin, powdered mint, pepper powder and coriander leaves to it. Mix well and add salt.
5. Then mix the fruits with the curd.
6. Add the crushed pomegranate seeds.
7. Serve chilled.

Raita with Greens

Ingredients

2 cups curd
½ cup skimmed milk
½ cup each of finely chopped spinach and coriander leaves
¼ cup mint leaves, chopped
1 tsp pomegranate seeds
¼ tsp sugar
1 green chilli, finely chopped
½ tsp cumin powder
1 tsp raisins
Salt to taste

Method

1. Wash the chopped greens and blanch in boiling water for 5 minutes.
2. Remove from the hot water and keep in chilled water till needed.
3. Whisk the curd, add the milk to it.
4. Add the rest of the ingredients except salt and mix well.
5. Take out the greens from the water and add to the curd. Add salt and mix well.
6. Serve chilled.

Fresh Fruit Raita

Ingredients

2 cups curd
¼ cup each of finely chopped apple and pineapple
¼ cup ripe banana, coarsely chopped
½ tsp pepper powder
¼ cup finely chopped capsicum
1 tsp cumin powder
1 green chilli, finely chopped
1 tbsp finely chopped seedless dates
1 tbsp coriander leaves
½ cup skimmed milk
Salt to taste

Method

1. Whisk the curd.
2. Add the rest of the ingredients to it along with the milk.
3. Mix well and serve chilled.

SNACKS

Open Carrot Sandwiches

Ingredients

12 slices of brown bread
1 cup each of grated carrots and cucumbers
1 tbsp grated cottage cheese
1 tsp each of green chilli paste or white pepper powder
2 tbsp finely chopped coriander leaves
¼ cup tomato sauce
½ tsp lime juice, Salt to taste

Method

1. Mix all the ingredients for the sandwich filling.
2. Apply the mixture on one side of the bread slices and cover with other bread slices. Serve chilled.

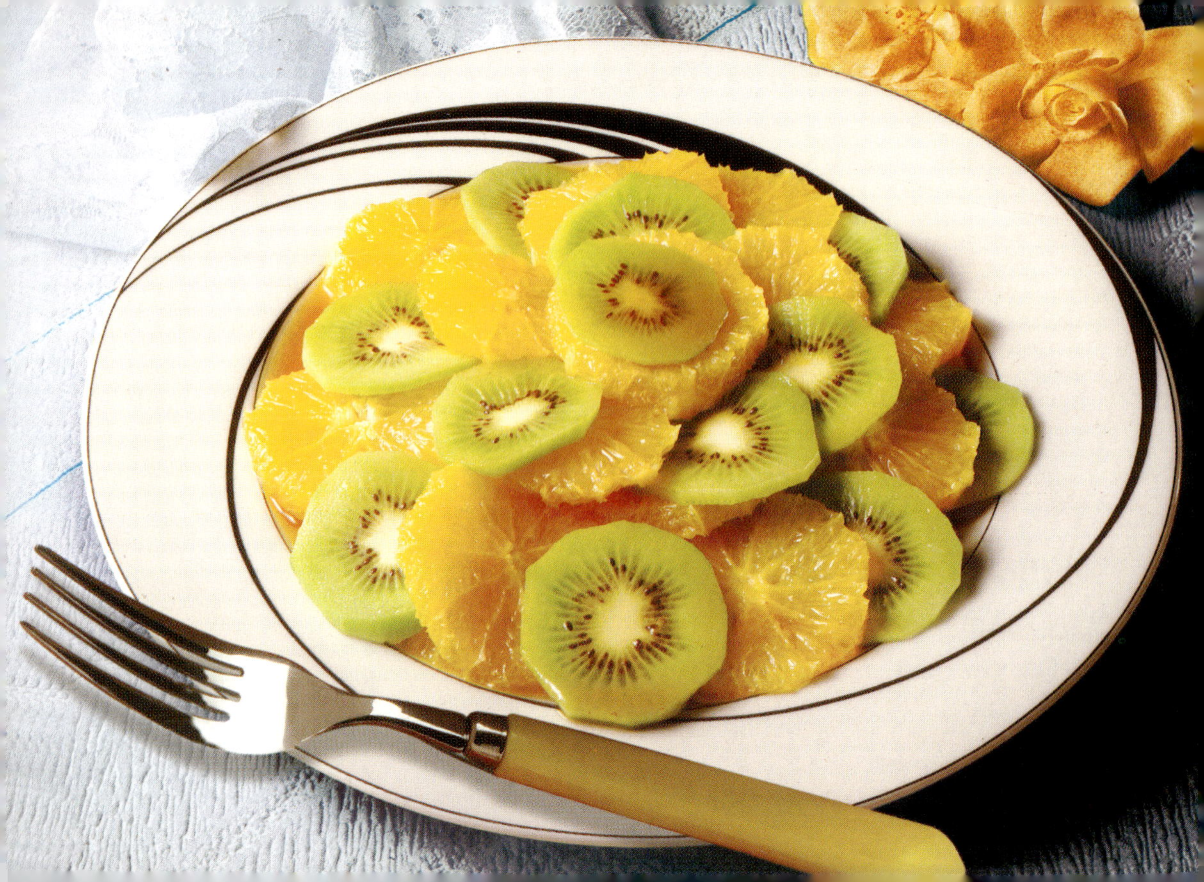

Fruit Delight

Ingredients

4 small oranges, peeled and sliced
2 kiwi fruits, peeled and sliced
2 tbsp soft brown sugar
2 tbsp white wine
½ tsp crushed cinnamon

Method

1. Arrange the oranges and kiwi fruits on a serving dish.
2. Sprinkle the sugar over the wine and stir until dissolved. Add the cinnamon and pour over the fruits. Serve.

←

Dal Pancakes

Ingredients

½ cup red dal
½ cup sprouted green gram
1 cup Bengal gram
¼ cup black gram
2 tbsp each of spinach puree and chopped onion
1 tsp green chilli paste
2 tbsp finely chopped coriander leaves
1 tbsp lime juice
2 tbsp ginger-garlic paste
2 tbsp oil
Salt to taste

Method

1. Wash and soak the lentils overnight.
2. Drain off the water and grind them coarsely.
3. Add the spinach puree, onion, green chilli paste, ginger-garlic paste, lime juice, coriander leaves and salt. Mix well.
4. Pour 1 teaspoon oil into a hot shallow pan. Take a ladleful of the batter and spread it evenly on the pan. Cook till it is golden brown in colour.
5. Flip over and cook on the other side.
6. Serve with mint or coconut chutney.

Coconut Chutney

Ingredients

1 cup grated coconut
1 tsp garlic paste
6 dry red chillies
1 tbsp lime juice
1 to 2 green chillies
Salt to taste

Method

1. Grind all the ingredients into a fine paste. This chutney can be served with *dosas, idlies* or rice.

Soya Pancakes

Ingredients

½ cup soya flour
1 cup wheat flour
¼ cup gram flour
½ cup grated onion
½ cup boiled and mashed potatoes
1 tbsp coriander leaves
1 tsp ginger paste
1 tsp each of cumin and chilli powder
A pinch of asafoetida
Salt and green chillies to taste

Method

1. Mix all the ingredients and make a batter of pouring consistency with water. Beat it well.
2. Heat the griddle. Take a ladleful of this batter and spread on the griddle in a circular motion.
3. Sprinkle some oil and cover it with a lid.
4. Turn it over to cook the other side.
5. Serve hot with coconut chutney.

Corn Sprouts Chat

Ingredients

1 cup each of sprouted green gram and boiled corn
1 cup curd, strained
1 tsp coarsely chopped coriander leaves
1 tsp chopped green chillies
1 tbsp each of mint and tamarind chutney
1 onion, finely chopped
1 potato, boiled and coarsely chopped
½ tsp cumin powder
1 tsp chilli powder
½ tsp black salt
Salt and pepper to taste

Method

1. Arrange the boiled corn and sprouted green gram on a serving plate.
2. Sprinkle the onion on top. Arrange the chopped potato on top of the onion.
3. Spread the curd over it. Sprinkle the dry *masalas* over it, followed by the mint chutney and tamarind chutney.
4. Sprinkle the green chillies and coriander leaves and serve immediately.

Corn Sprouts Chat (pg.107) →

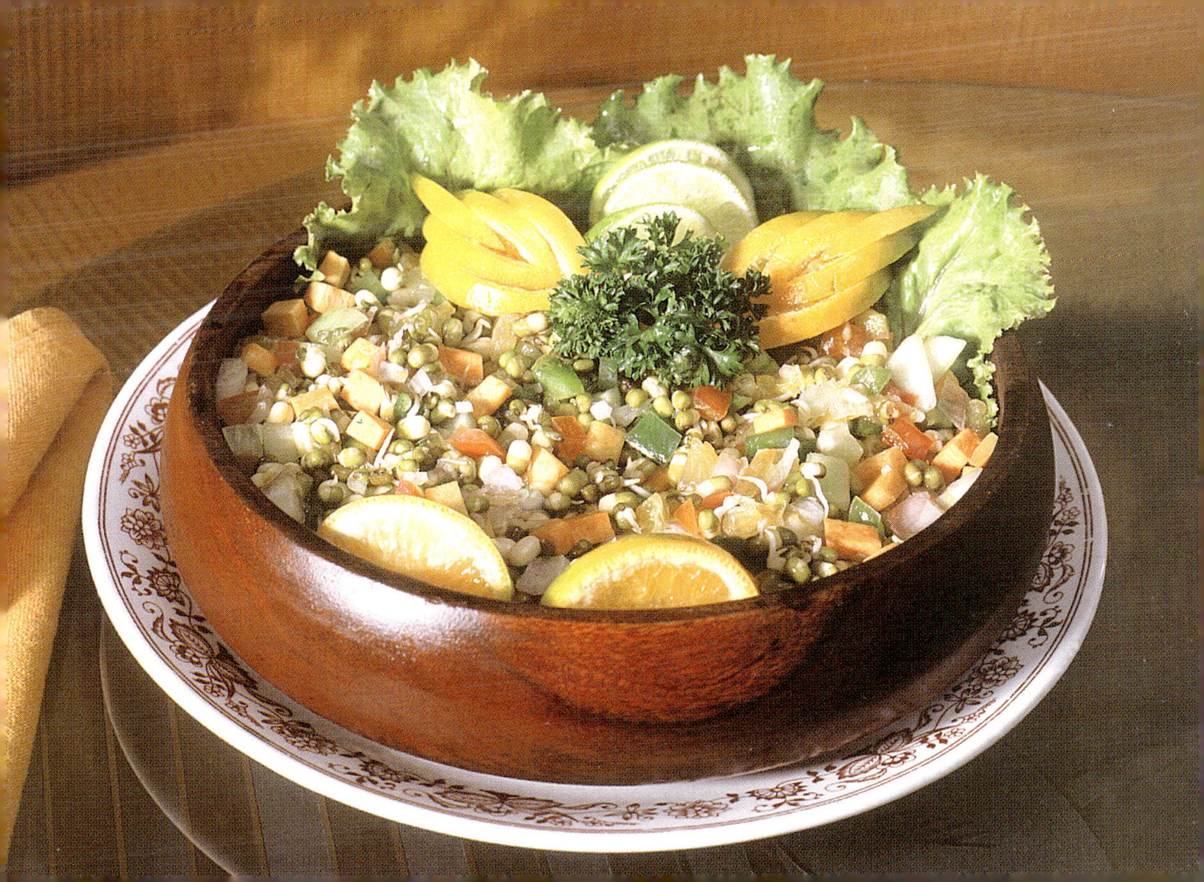

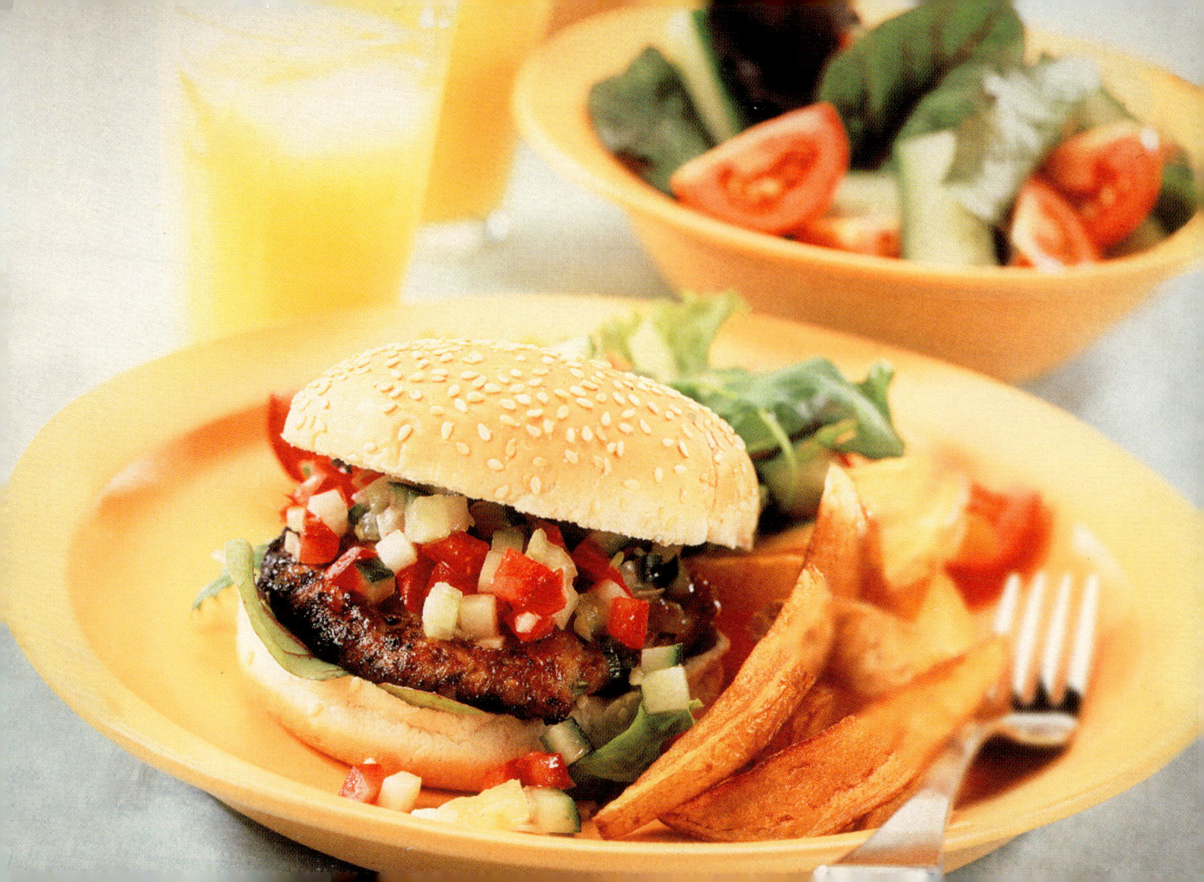

Burger Supreme

Ingredients

Wheat flour buns (brown bread)
1 cup boiled and chopped mixed vegetables
2 tomatoes (1 cut into rounds and 1 diced)
1 each of cucumber and onion, cut into rounds
1 tsp each of ginger paste, garlic paste and lime juice
1 tbsp green chilli paste
2 tbsp tomato sauce
1 tbsp each of chilli sauce, mustard sauce and oil
1 cucumber, diced, A few lettuce leaves
Breadcrumbs as required
Salt and pepper to taste

Method

1. Mix the vegetables (leaving aside 2 tablespoons) with the ginger, garlic, green chilli paste, lime juice and salt. Blend in a blender.
2. Add the breadcrumbs and shape them into round cutlets.
3. Pour the oil into a non-stick frying pan. Then fry each cutlet till light brown in colour.
4. Slice each bun into half.
5. Arrange the lettuce leaves on one portion of the bun. Then apply a little tomato sauce, mustard sauce and chilli sauce on it. Arrange a tomato slice over it, and then place a cutlet on top of the tomato slice. Cover the cutlet with slices of cucumber and onion. Finally spread some of the diced vegetables.
6. Cover with the other half of the bun and serve immediately with French fries.

Corn Chat

Ingredients

6 fresh corn cobs
1 cup finely chopped onions
1 tsp finely chopped green chillies
1 tsp sweet tamarind chutney
½ cup grated coconut
1 tbsp crushed peanuts
2 tbsp finely chopped coriander
Salt to taste

Method

1. Pressure cook the fresh corn cobs with salt in 4 cups of water for 5 minutes, after the first whistle.
2. Cool and remove the corn from the cobs.
3. Mix the corn with the onions, coconut, peanuts, green chillies and salt. Keep aside.
4. At the time of serving, pour the chutney over the mixture and mix well.
5. Serve chilled, garnished with the coriander.

Paneer Sandwiches

Ingredients

1 cup cottage cheese, cut into tiny cubes
¼ cup finely chopped tomatoes (seeds removed)
¼ cup finely chopped capsicum
¼ cup tinned corn
1 tsp lime juice
2 tbsp grated cheese
1 tbsp milk
12 slices of bread
Salt and pepper to taste

Method

1. Remove the crusts from the bread slices.
2. Mix all the ingredients. Spread the mixture on one of the bread slice.
3. Cover with another bread slice.
4. Do this with the other slices of bread. Cut into desired shapes.
5. Serve with chutney or tomato sauce.

Note: Keep wrapped in a damp cloth until served.

Paneer Corn Delight

Ingredients

1 cup cottage cheese, crumbled
1 cup boiled baby corns
½ cup finely chopped onions
1 tsp chopped ginger
1 tbsp lime juice
1 tsp vinegar
1 tsp pomegranate seeds
2 tsp each of pepper and cumin powder
2 tbsp chopped coriander leaves
Salt and pepper to taste

Method

1. Mix the crumbled cottage cheese and boiled corns and keep aside.
2. Mix the onion, ginger, lime juice, vinegar and all the dry *masalas*.
3. Add the cottage cheese-corn mixture to it.
4. Mix well and garnish with the coriander leaves.
5. Serve.

Rava Dhokla

Ingredients

½ cup semolina
¾ cup sour curd
¼ tsp ginger paste
1 tbsp coriander leaves
1 tbsp grated coconut
1 tsp each of sugar and mustard seeds
1 tsp finely chopped green chillies
2 tsp oil
1 tsp Eno fruit salt
Salt to taste

Method

1. Mix the sour curd and semolina thoroughly and keep aside for 2 hours.
2. Add the ginger paste, sugar and salt.
3. At the time of steaming, add the fruit salt and beat well.
4. Grease small moulds with 1 teaspoon oil and pour the batter into them. Steam for half an hour.
5. Remove from the fire and cool.
6. Heat 1 teaspoon oil and fry the mustard seeds and chopped green chillies for a few seconds.
7. Sprinkle this seasoning over the *dhoklas*, and serve garnished with coconut and coriander leaves.